Settling St. Malo

http://ulpress.org
University of Louisiana at Lafayette Press
P.O. Box 43558
Lafayette, LA 70504-3558

Printed in the United States

Library of Congress Cataloging-in-Publication Data

Names: Gonzales, Randy (Randy Eugene), 1968- author.
Title: Settling St. Malo Randy Gonzales.
Description: Lafayette, LA : University of Louisiana at Lafayette Press,
    2023.
Identifiers: LCCN 2023012216 | ISBN 9781959569039 (paperback)
Subjects: LCSH: Filipino Americans--Louisiana--Poetry. |
    Louisiana--History--19th century--Poetry. | Louisiana--History--20th
    century--Poetry. | Barataria Bay (La.)--Poetry. | New Orleans
    (La.)--Poetry. | LCGFT: Documentary poetry.
Classification: LCC PS3607.O549 S48 2023 | DDC 811/.6--dc23/eng/20230424
LC record available at https://lccn.loc.gov/2023012216

Settling St. Malo

RANDY GONZALES

2023
UNIVERSITY OF LOUISIANA AT LAFAYETTE PRESS

Nola

St. Malo

Barataria Bay

ACKNOWLEDGMENTS

A version of "A Filipino American Life in Letters to/from US Institutions" originally appeared in *Proceedings from the Document Academy* as "(Un)Documented, a Narrative of M— in Letters to/from US Institutions"; versions of "Get Your Father from the Bar" and "Become" appeared in my dissertation *Filipino, Too: Compositions on Culture and Identity*; a version of "Become" appeared in *Redactions*; a version of "Do-bo" appeared in the *Philippine Star* and *The Ultimate Filipino Adobo Cookbook* by Claude Tayag; and reading of an excerpt from "When Manilamen Fished at St. Malo (1840s–1906)" was part of the public art project *Disappearing St. Malo, 2022* by Cheyenne Concepcion.

My doctoral work at the University of Southern Mississippi was significant in my journey to discover and write about my cultural heritage. Special thanks to Jeffrey Kaufmann, who taught me to think like an anthropologist; Linda Pierce Allen, who gave me the critical lens to read Filipino America; Angela Ball, Rebecca Morgan Frank, and Steve Barthelme, who each contributed to making me a better writer.

I would like to thank all that engaged me in conversations about Filipino and Louisiana culture, especially my life partner, Arleen Gonzales, who patiently endures my questions about the Philippines and Filipino culture; my brother, Edward Gonzales, who teaches me about fishing and coastal Louisiana; and Carolyn "Caggy" Thiel, who shares her memories of our Filipino family.

When my interest in this project waned, the members of the Philippine Louisiana Historical Society, especially Robert Romero, reminded me how important it is for me to share my story. I am thankful for their friendship and community.

I would like to offer a thanks to Marina Espina, Rhonda Richoux, and Carmelo Astilla for the work they have done to share the story of Filipino Louisiana. And Michael Salgarolo and Winston Ho for being generous collaborators. Their research has made my work better. Thanks to Charlie Serigne, Morgan Christie, and Devon Lord for editing the collection and for the family of Fonville Winans for permission to include a photograph of Manila Village. Thanks to the University of Louisiana at Lafayette and Dr. Mary Ann Wilson for the financial support I receive as holder of the Dr. James Wilson/BORSF Eminent Scholar Endowed Professorship in Southern Studies.

Finally, I would like to acknowledge the consistent support of my family—my mother, Fay Gonzales Vogt, wife, Arleen, siblings—Gay, Edward, Rhonda, and Ronell—and my sons—Kyle and Del. This is our story.

TABLE OF CONTENTS

For Evelyn Guillera Gonzales Planchard (my grandmother), and her children (*left to right*) Ronald (my father), Diane, and Howard, and all those who have questioned the significance of their Filipino American story.

Cultural Memory

she liked to tell of my teenage father
who drove her Mercury into a streetlight
she chased him with a stick or bat
or just a fist down the street

when she talked about love
Enrique wore a deep green suit
"Snakey" a term of endearment for
the way he slides and sways to the music
"your grandpa could really dance"

you had to coax the years from her
to go beyond the bookkeeper
"don't need no damn
computer to keep the books"

stories she wore best
recalled Evelyn the welder
single mom with three young children
works at the shipyard doing what
she can for a world at war

she struggled to remember
the Filipino Colony Bar
dances at the Italian Hall
resisted descriptions of her baro't saya
or the youthful enthusiasm
of tossing paper flowers into a screaming crowd

she talked about Filipinos as if recounting
a history that didn't include her
"that's what a Filipino guy told mama"
"Filipinos would all gather for weekend dances"
so did she

1

we must account for this slippage
make sense of her at my father's school
offering her complexion as evidence
of his whiteness to counter
brown on his birth certificate

map those memories
on histories that include us
St. Malo
Manila Village
Filipino Colony Bar

understand
immigration
migration
labor
policy
segregation
marginalization
assimilation
as conceptions
of our erasure

restore what we can
from fragments
of cultural memory

St. Malo

When Manilamen Fished at St. Malo (1840s–1906)

I. St. Malo (1883)
bayou
village
island with no clear western shore
patches of marsh
lagoons and canals
unraveling into the Gulf

from the lake you see miles
of flooded rushes laid out
before a chenier—narrow ridge
sand and shell plowed up by storm
surges—forested with live oaks

until you clear slash of wind-sculpted
willows do you notice stilted structures
where men have claimed patches of marsh

from the lake the landscape is all Louisiana
wet prairie of swaying sawgrass
cane scratching into low clouds
scatter of poule d'eau
darting teal still frames
of egrets postured in shallows

plain of water ripples
as shrimp pop from
the course of pursuing redfish

past the mouth the bayou turns *Asiatic*
hat-shaped eaves strung with smoked fish
cocks clamoring at domed cages
squat men examining seines

mile after mile more cypress
buildings all stained in moss
more fishermen tending to tasks
without a nod to your passing

II. I don't know
what registers in the ship's log —
one Tagalog overboard
Malay slipped out at last
light dispersed Indio scouts
along grassy coast

I know some seamen
once on some vessel
Spanish or not somehow
found their way to the southern
shore of Lake Borgne

I don't know how
they found St. Malo

perhaps astride stray
cypress logs wise
to tidal shifts and false bayous

with the help of gentle guides
singing tales of Juan St. Malo
or aboard abandoned pirogues
adrift on Bayou La Loutre

I don't know who
with water-logged feet
walked through shivs
of broken cane
built a village
on secondhand accounts

planted palmetto rooftops
over the ledge of the lake

I know they lived on the lake
through the storms of 1843
56 60 93 until 1906
when the last were tossed
with nets oars timber
from piers submerged
balconies all cast bit
by bit out to sea

nothing remained
but tales of *Orientals*
living in the lake
thrifty Malays
blowing across
the Gulf behind
alligator hide sails

I don't know how many
were buried in the marsh
how many rolled up in waves
swept from slumber
fallen overboard dragged
down tangled in debris
lost to the diseases of the day
or the violence of other men

I know they built and rebuilt
from thatched island huts
to stilted cypress structures
lifted themselves above
fished and lived full sails
away from city society

I know some stayed

why

ask any South Louisiana
man who leaves his family
each weekend chases trout
and redfish around a lake
waits on ducks to light
on the mirror of a morning pond
why
he'll say "to get away"

we don't know what
"from it all" meant
to the Manilamen

but it was enough

got them this far
and kept them

III. Manilamen (1840s)
pioneers of a Gulf border
fishermen of fields more
than a day away

settled uncontested
amphibious land
built palmetto huts
simple fishing camp

sustained by the lake
and what could be bartered
with captains who sailed
their catch to market

IV. St. Malo (1840s)
station in the dream
of a passable land bridge
to bypass the Mississippi
connect NOLA
to a deepwater port
at the island end
of St. Bernard Parish
by train first to Bayou
St. Malo then across
the marsh to the Gulf's edge
promises of coastal trade
extensive wharves
commodious warehouses
along the lake's southern shore

V. Manilamen (1860s)
fished all along
Lake Borgne's southern shore
around Malheureux Point
into the Chandeleur Sound
in the grand marshes
about Elephant Pass

returned to St. Malo
full bottoms

met luggers
sorted sold and iced
three sheepshead or redfish
for 15 cents a bunch

primary seafood supplier
of city markets

fishermen and hunters
of lower St. Bernard
supplied NOLA
almost exclusively with fish
shrimp oysters and game
via the Mexican Gulf Railroad —
didn't reach the goal
of Ninemile Bayou
or even St. Malo
terminated instead
at Proctorville

better for the Manilamen
more comfortable living
one stop further than most

the Spanish (Catalans mostly)
could fish from Proctorville

Manilamen would stay
closer to the source

VI. to city eyes just fishermen
of uncertain ethnicity
men who lived by hook and net

of a group that came in a trickle
not in immigrant waves
like the ships full of Acadiens
Isleños Germans and Croatians
who settled designated spaces
or later like Irish Chinese Italians
dispersed by labor demands

arrived a few at a time
steady stream of single men

stepping away from a seaman's life
settling where others wouldn't
mingling in coastal margins

even when they married white
few perceived them as a threat

VII. Lafcadio Hearn (1883)
"discovers" a *Malay* village
transported to the marsh whole cloth
minus the rule and order of Spain
minus women (an absence engendering
morbid curiosity if not envy)

Hearn wrote upon the urban fear
of wetlands the unpredictable
storms insects and alligators
and anyone sturdy enough
to inhabit such a wilderness

"civil society" perpetuated
the lore of *uncivilized Malays*
told of men who'd tie you to a stake
so mosquitoes and green-headed
horse flies could suck at your flesh

some claimed stakes mere effect
mosquitoes the real threat
not your average insect
an intelligent species
trained to attack
those of a lighter
complexion

first the customs agent
then tax collectors and of course
anyone who would fish their waters

a sting meant a fever
of the rankest kind
if not death
a clear warning
never to return

VIII. seafarers
from the Philippines
men in the world
before the world
would call us Filipinos

even those raised
outside capital walls
preferred Manilamen
over *unchristened*
Malays or *Lascars*
over *Chinamen*

even those of North
Asian ancestry
preferred to be
men from Manila
if their preference
Hispano Filipinos
was not echoed

a colonial mentality
for the New World

men once resistant
to Spanish authority
and influence now
assert assimilative
features of a shared God
and speaking Spanish

like everyone else
down in St. Bernard Parish

XI. St. Malo (1883)
Fourteen sturdy bunkhouses
enough for 150 fishermen
lined Bayou St. Malo

a base
for excursions
further down the coast

luggers loaded with
crackers
coffee
sugar
beans and rice
battered pots
a charcoal furnace
rolls of wind-torn canvas

enough to survive
a temporary encampment
until the lugger
sat low on its lines

only then
would they open
sails to St. Malo
to deliver their catch

XII. no different
than most
Louisiana fishermen
seamen accustomed

to shifting from ship
to port settling
for opportunities
sailing off when
welcomes end

those who stayed
sent for their kabayan

letters written at St. Malo
handed off in Vera Cruz
passed along mountain
trails to Acapulco
pocketed until
Manila or Cebu

the message "come
find Filipino villages
along the Louisiana coast"
not just delivered

believed
and enacted

XIII. Yellow Fever (1883)
residents fled to Proctorville
when yellow fever
swept through NOLA
to breathe the unspoiled air

they camped on banks
near tall native grasses
mosquitoes favored for shade

Proctorville was the town
you'd go for a day or two
from the city to hunt fish

dip a toe in cool lake waters
eat at the freshest oyster stalls
cruise around Lake Borgne

although just a few miles east
no steamer ventured to St. Malo

captains steered wide
of the shifting shore
the unmoored islands
and mud-spit inlets

heeded warnings of reeds
clattering long lances
toward the lapping lake

XIV. not just Bayou St. Malo
Manilamen scattered all along the southern shore
setting up short-lived encampments
in scrub willows
on low grassy islands

just deep enough in the marsh
to spare boats the persistent
chop of the shallow lake

lived with little but the basics —
shelter boats and nets
good knife sturdy deck of cards
moss-filled sacks to sleep upon

XV. not all fishermen
some were captains
invested in boats and seines
of them a few

like Hilario and Seraphino
built great bayou casas

successful entrepreneurs
managed a *Malay* fishing fleet
housed crews in St. Malo bunkhouses

in the 60s broke a Spanish
monopoly on NOLA markets
gained a competitive advantage
by living in the fishing grounds

grew rich

not just in fish

Steve Martin(ez)
possessed mysterious
influence over the marsh's
fur-bearing mammals
able to snare them
when others failed

made him the wealthiest
Manilaman on the lake

XVII. Great Gulf Storm (1893)
Lake Borgne flowed over the marsh
the whole island submerged
stilts not high enough
waves crash through windows
boats just float away

some survive

screech into the moonless night
as the lake laps at rooftops

the storm descends
from the northeast
accelerates
across the marsh
pushes lake water
clear to the Gulf

more than half
downriver of NOLA drown
not a single child
in the worst hit areas
survives

fittest young men mainly
escape on improvised rafts
unwavering grip on life
ride fifteen-foot swells
crash with everyday
buoyant debris

whole families washed away
names never pronounced again

some survive

farmhand carries
his wife and two children
through waist-deep waters
slips falls
won't let go

at St. Malo Marshal Marcelino
tethered to his second-story
home tows seven villagers to safety

they huddle for three days
atop sacks of swelling rice

wait for the lake
to recede to its basin

watch as it reveals
what they've lost

XIX. Last Storm (1906)
as stories of the last storm
migrated further from the source
plans abound to extend the rails to St. Malo
for sportsmen to access *the best* duck hunting
in the state and leisure seekers
to soak in brackish lagoons

nothing comes of these plans
but about 100 Manilamen
reclaim St. Malo
build a modest fishing camp
enough of a presence
to stoke local lore
about *refugees*
from justice

then again
a storm

all are gone

perished

or just had
enough

XX. if you're looking for St. Malo now
forget the slender supports
lifting shelters above the marsh

they're gone

you'll see reeds
sway on receding
clumps of land

look out over a lagoon
instead of a lake

you'll find pilings
just above the waterline
at Janhcke's Ditch

you can imagine
these barnacled
stumps once held
cypress homes
or once a pier
strung with seines
perhaps Valentine or
any of the other youth
raised at St. Malo
ran on the wavy limbs
of the remaining live oak

perhaps perched
on the ridge
they tracked
the parting
swamp grass

even before levees
and dredging disrupted

the flow of sediment
to the patchy shore

before the surrounding marsh
subsided into the lake
the shell embankment
rose above the reeds

whether Manilamen
made use of mollusks
to firm sinking soil
or the Chitimacha
before them
mounded rangia clams

they built a place
to steady steps
when breathless
energy of water
overwhelmed any sense
they belonged at sea

The *Times-Democrat* expedition to St. Malo in 1883 resulted in two
feature articles, which would become the primary sources of most
accounts of the Filipino village, one written by Charles Whitney
distributed locally in the *Times-Democrat* and one written by
Lafcadio Hearn distributed nationally in the *Harper's Weekly*.

Local articles focused on the southern shore of Lake Borgne, not
the *Malay settlement*, provide insight into how Louisiana residents
understood the Filipino presence.

Lafcadio Hearn and company depart St. Malo. *Harper's Weekly*, March 31, 1883.

Rediscovered

St. Malo rose over the marshy plain
in 1883 a new American discovery
of a Filipino village of sturdy cypress
buildings along a remote bayou

rediscovered again twenty years later
perhaps no geographers or historians in the US
even know Louisiana contains a Filipino community

at the time at least 2,000
Filipinos in South Louisiana
not forgotten
not invisible
not assimilated
just not readily absorbed
into America's narrow
narrative of itself

St. Malo rediscovered again in the 1980s
when Marina Espina's community history
reminded us to look past dominant
narratives to ask who's documented
whose perspective and what's
being prepped for memory

now when you discover St. Malo
be mindful of the Manilamen
the vague outline of fishermen
leaning over the porch rail
consider their perspective
be wary of visitors
interested in them as
economy or architecture
of writers who sail away
to tell their stories

Sourced language (*in italics*) from a *Courier-Journal* (Louisville)
article that looked to Filipino American fishermen in Louisiana
for insight into *what sort of people* US soldiers were fighting in the
Philippine-American War.

Marina Espina's *Filipinos in Louisiana* (1988) places Filipinos at St.
Malo in the *mid-eighteenth century*, circa 1765, a date that settled
Filipinos in the United States before the Declaration of Indepen-
dence, a compelling, but unsupported claim that gets reasserted
each time someone discovers St. Malo.

Historical Significance

the first documented permanent Filipino settlement
established in the United States on bayou St. Malo
which was *propitious land for the maintenance of human life*
meaning a stand of live oak bayous abounding in fish
bays and inlets with extensive oyster beds
ponds teeming with teal dry prairies attracting snipe
maze of unmapped bayous perfect for Juan St. Malo
to establish a base for Maroons
in search of refuge from the barbarity of the plantation
we can imagine Manilamen
slipping out to the sparsely inhabited marsh
after 1785 after Spanish troops
spread across the wetlands in search of St. Malo (the man)
killed him and drove his followers to Barataria Bay
not sooner
not 1762 when Spain acquired Louisiana from the French
not 1778 when Canary Islanders settled St. Bernard
Manilamen settled St. Malo after it was known
named and racialized built just south of *Negro Lagoon*
on the bayou named after the Maroon leader
location so perfect it's difficult to imagine
it wasn't utilized by the Chitimacha years earlier
after the French pushed them into the swamps
if not a permanent settlement seasonally populated
before and after threats of summer storms

Filipinos built palmetto palm huts on the bayou's natural levees
sometime before the storm of 1843
washed away first-hand accounts
not until after the Civil War
would they build above the average storm surge
construct durable cypress structures able to house
up to 150 fishermen buildings meant to last yet unlikely
to withstand a few dozen hurricane seasons
not just on bayou St. Malo

Filipinos fished all around what some called "Malay Louisiana"
settled the whole peninsula
lived simply on ridges and marsh islands
in structures as temporary as most fishermen

but St. Malo was the base
the Filipino space described by Lafcadio Hearn
and sketched by JO Davidson in 1883
the village imagined in NOLA fish markets
talked about in galleys of seagoing vessels
the home of men whose stories have been forgotten
the place documented through the imagination of travelers
and journalists recalled in community memory
historicized and mythologized
all of us looking for our history
peer out to this horizon
through the fog
see an outline
a distinct shape
significant from
what we learned
we call it St. Malo

Because the history of St. Malo is Louisiana history too.

When the Manilamen Demanded Justice (1860)

a few dozen Filipinos from NOLA
descended on St. Bernard Parish

after Spanish fishermen
threatened by the presence
of Filipino fishermen surrounded
and shot two delivering
fish to Proctorville

not the first left to hasty graves
but the last to be overlooked

Filipinos marched on the courthouse
(early instance of Filipino American protest)
demanded Judge Toca issue a warrant
made it clear they would no longer tolerate
the wink and nod of parish officials

Filipino fishermen had the vocal support
of business-minded folks who imagined
cheaper seafood without a Spanish monopoly

yet the mutilated bodies remained on the beach
for a week until Filipinos from NOLA arrived
to encourage the coroner to attend to the corpses

not *transient Malays* established Filipinos
of all ages fishermen businessmen
entrepreneurs and their educated sons

numbers to influence
voice to demand action

Spanish fishermen afraid of retribution
or justice dispersed into the marsh

the judge urged the sheriff
to capture the accused

the community made sure of it
two Spanish fishermen

an Italian accomplice
arrested within a week

Filipino fishermen returned
to the business of developing
the local seafood industry

Times-Picayune, New Orleans Daily Crescent, Sunday Delta, and *Daily Delta* all reported on the August 1860 conflict between Filipino and Spanish fishermen, some thought Filipinos were Chinese, all supported bringing more *smaller and choicer* fish to market.

In October, the *New Orleans Daily Crescent* reported that the accused were acquitted, the *Crescent* emphasized the impact the conflict had on NOLA diets. They didn't report on how Filipinos reacted to the news.

Arrivals

Manilamen like most Louisiana
settlers sailed here
but not as passengers
seamen who decided not to return
to their vessels instead
sailed out to fishing villages
joined a fishing crew for room and board
and a little cash for a day in the city
some made themselves at home
some quickly back to the port
familiar story of seamen of any nationality
Louisiana in the nineteenth century encouraged immigration
needed labor for marshes
post-Civil War for the sugarcane harvest
no need to document
no immigration quotas to restrict
a state in need of a population welcoming all who would labor
yet the arrival of Manilamen told in more dramatic terms
they *jumped ship ran away*
desperate refugees from Spanish justice
deserters from Spanish ships
many reneged on terms of employment
some like Albert Navarro escaped literal chains
the Filipino who worked the Atlantic slave trade as a boy
had to escape and seek refuge in the marsh
but for each story of escape we have a planned migration
Augustin Feliciano a petty officer in the Spanish Navy
retired and set sail for New Orleans in 1807
or the Traje brothers who left the Philippines as passengers
intent on settling in Louisiana
not all leave because of terrible conditions onboard
Felipe Madrigal left his position for an Irish bride
yet each Filipino arrival described as *jumping ship*
avoid the phrase even if most left their vessels
before fulfilling their contracts

avoid the dramatic effect
when you emphasize the leaving you focus on terms of employment
decentralize the Manilamen from their story
abandon them to the reporters and history makers
who identify them as labor
who describe them as *runaways* and *deserters*
precursors of *illegal* and *undocumented*
rhetorical markers to emphasize the untrustworthiness
of non-white immigrants who like other settlers
were just looking for an opportunity
or perhaps America is a nation of runaways
every settler running from something
desperate and willing to forcibly unsettle those in their path
certainly not our national narrative
settlement is not sold as escape
nor the displacement of Native people
it was packaged at least to Europeans as a dream
pursuit of happiness opportunity to be free
a message Manilamen may have distrusted
aware that *Malays* didn't fit neatly into racial hierarchies of the state
perhaps to some this explained why they ran to the swamp
every city-bound resident might ask who
but a *desperate refugee* would disembark in NOLA
and decide to settle in the marsh of course
the ethnically ambiguous brown people would be on the run
need to settle in an abandoned Maroon hideout
remoteness sells the narrative of escape
if the Manilamen are victims the Spanish perfect villains
no need to blame American political or social structures
when the Spanish exacted heavy taxes and forced enlistment
who wouldn't try to escape their authority
Manilamen when not trading on their own Hispanic traits
would certainly play up Spanish abuses
both can be true
they couldn't stay in the Philippines
sailed to Louisiana and disembarked
minus the drama of a furtive departure

they asked where to find other Filipinos
heard of St. Malo or Manila Village
even if in haste knew what they wanted
what they were walking away from
in this regard no more desperate than anyone
else who sees an opportunity and jumps at it

The 1883 articles described Filipinos as *runaways*, *deserters*, and
criminals, biased descriptors reprinted in 1898–99 with the surge of
national attention that followed US annexation of the Philippines.

In the twentieth century, local newspapers and community
members repeated biased descriptors as if they were unbiased
historical fact.

Now . . .

NOLA

A communal space, Bulbancha, "place of many tongues,"
where Native peoples—Choctaw, Chitimacha, Houma—
traded with each other, and later the colonizers
who would claim and rename it *La Nouvelle-Orléans*.

The Filipino Community in the 1935 ELKS Krewe of Orleanians parade.
Christopher Valley Sr. Papers, Louisiana Historical Center, New Orleans
Jazz Museum.

Filipino Mardi Gras

Granny scanned the photograph
pointed "That's Fe Fe"
at the girl with her chin raised
over the Filipino flag

she remembered men going down to Chef Menteur
to cut the cane for the frame of the float
remembered them constructing it in front
of her father's bar dressing as a Filipina
with a wide-shouldered shirt
and ankle-length skirt type of clothes
she would've worn to church or a fiesta
if she had lived in the Philippines

remembered masquerading
like those who wore the sad white-painted face of the Pierrot
the flirtatious French maid's outfits
the red-yawn hair of Raggedy Ann
paradegoers who waved and encouraged flowers
saw an *oriental* maiden from a tropical island
too simple a costume for Mardi Gras
couldn't compete with the bold colors of the Russian Cossacks
or the fur clad French Canadian woodsmen on the US Forest Service float
not nearly as delightful as the harlequins
as colorful as the George Washingtons
or as absurd as the white women masquerading as *Chinamen*

now we recognize
in their design
the internal conflict

living with two flags
one held by Juan de la Cruz
the Filipino everyman
the other by a US Navy sailor

Uncle Sam the white-bearded symbol
of imperialism occupies the float
as he does the Philippines

in their tropical scene he is armed
with a giant pair of scissors
a policy critique dulled by the smile
of the chained Filipino maiden

the scene framed by the mestizo youth
who by parading in the all-white
Mardi Gras highlight the community's
assimilative properties

"Me, Fe, and Nita. We all rode."
the whole family involved
from finance to refreshments
to flower-making committees

"that was a long time ago
I don't know why you care
what we did back then"

maybe if I hadn't
seen them in a book
seen community
pride

I wouldn't have
recognized her past
as my history

not just her story
but our story
our history

I wouldn't have cared

Shaped by conversations with my grandmother more than seventy years after the parade rolled.

Enhanced with details found in articles from *The Sunday Item-Tribune* and *Times-Picayune*, the 1935 ELKS Krewe of Orleanians' registration files, and Espina's *Filipinos in Louisiana*.

Missing details about the role of my great-grandfather, the Caballeros de Dimas-Alang leader who registered the float, but who died before anyone considered his story important enough to collect.

Guide to Local Filipino Organizations

I. Overview
when you read *put on by the local Filipino society*
they could be referencing a number of overlapping
organizations with shared membership
but slightly different missions

Filipino Communities of America welcomed all
to learn about policies impacting Filipino residents
and to be entertained by string orchestras

Louisiana Lodge No. 34 of Caballeros de Dimas-Alang
integrated the national organization's mission with NOLA culture
designed a Philippine independence themed Mardi Gras float

Filipino American Circle educated youth
who'd dance the cariñosa at international days

Kapisanan Filipino Society celebrated José Rizal
with recitations of his work and stereopticon views of his home

each organization represented the community

each sustained it

II. Kasamahan
est. La Union Philipina (18??)
to nurture ethnic bonds
secured cemetery vaults
so St. Malo fishermen could
rest in eternal community

est. Hispano Filipino
Benevolent Society (1870)
to aid Filipinos

in times of need
when you can't care
for yourself (illness
death) or your own
(disaster) for new
arrivals emptied yet
eager from the Philippines
provide a sustaining network
(support and opportunity)
where to go and who to see

III. Bayanihan
hosted a calico ball
to contribute as part
of a larger community
wore plain cotton
dresses and suits
some homemade
for this one occasion
to donate to those
more needy
give back
thank the city
for its welcome

IV. José Rizal Day (1912–1930s)
one of those men
produced only once
poet scholar patriot

novels to stoke a revolution
forge a Filipino identity
in Spanish in opposition
to Spanish authority

shot for treason (1896)
his martyrdom
another match
for the cause

every man woman
child recited his words
until Spain was defeated

in NOLA Kapisanan
Filipino celebrates
José Rizal Day each year
with songs recitations
in Tagalog Spanish
and English

honoring Rizal's life and death
in the land of the latest colonizer

to reinforce an independent spirit
within a Filipino American community
at home in a nation that celebrates liberty
yet selectively denies it

Kasamahan—bonds within the Filipino American community, the
parties and dances talked about in oral histories, the shared burial
site at St. Vincent De Paul Cemetery No 2.

Bayanihan—connections, contributions to NOLA society, evident
in *Times-Democrat* and *Times-Picayune* coverage of public events
hosted by Filipino organizations.

Enrique Gonzalez (my grandfather) at his naturalization ceremony on
June 13, 1947. Author's private collection.

Status Updates

I. Manilamen (?–1899)
no homogenous Louisiana
whoever will endure
wetlands and the weather
welcomed to stay and labor

II. Spain cedes the Philippines (1898)
to the United States
whether Filipinos like it or not

conflict — Philippine-American War
1899–1902 (over 200,000 civilians die) —
paired with benevolent assimilation
to educate the Filipinos and uplift
and civilize and Christianize them
Catholic not Christian enough
according to President McKinley (1902)

rhetoric that leaves no logical
legal mechanisms to deny Filipinos
US entry and residence
only citizenship

the term "national of the United States"
means a person who though not a citizen
owes the United States permanent allegiance

Manilamen (US national 1899)
approved for government jobs
feel free to move families
around Louisiana or beyond

in California Spkr. Henderson (1902)
pushes aside nativists fears

not a single Filipino in the country
not one in any of our forty-five States

while in Louisiana the Filipino population
grows to over 2,000

Filipino (US national 1899–1934)
migrate to the States
join the US Navy (1908+)
study in America (1903+)
labor and move to ethnic centers
like Louisiana
show your allegiance and labor
have an American family
assimilate accordingly and labor
feel free to labor
feel like you belong in America
like you are more than your labor
parade your allegiance

nothing less expected

expect nothing more

III. Tydings-McDuffie Act (1934)
guarantees the Philippines independence
and immediately reclassifies Filipinos
from US nationals to resident aliens

Filipinos in NOLA (alien)
yes to independence
no to liminal status

resident yet unable to enter
able to leave but not return

the term "Filipino" means a person
who cannot become a US citizen

Filipino Communities of America (1936)
seeks the city's cooperation
advocates for citizenship
for Filipinos living as Americans

join us
hear our witnesses
listen to our orchestra
watch our children
sing of our assimilation

note our allegiance

we follow American
traditions marry
Americans have citizen
children we've lived
subject to American law
for over thirty years
only now to be denied
what we've enjoyed

the term "alien" means
one who doesn't belong

Filipino (alien 1934)
stay stateside
wait for policy
to favor you

Filipino Repatriation Act (1935)
go back to the Philippines
we'll pay for your ticket

the term "Asian" means
one who should go home

to: President Theodore Roosevelt
from: Filipino Seaman's Association

discrimination toward us has increased
since the Merchant Marine Act (1936)
our employability limited
our unions have removed us
once loyal subjects now aliens
some of us served in the US Navy
joined the Emergency Fleet in WWI
American all but on paper
now a *security threat*
treated as foreign seamen
when we have lived
legally honestly
in Louisiana most of our lives

IV. Filipino (alien 1938)
document your arrival

the above-named man
(Jose Umadhay)
arrived in San Francisco
September 19, 1914
aboard the USAT Sheridan

V. Luce-Cellar Act (1946)
cuts the chains
Filipinos in the US
before 1934 eligible
for citizenship

Filipino (alien 1946)
redeclare your allegiance

petition for naturalization
wait patiently

the term "naturalized" means
you're no longer an "alien"
(you're still an "Asian")

hundreds in NOLA
naturalized ASAP

VI. Enrique put on his best suit
(June 13, 1947) not everyday
a man changes his status
anticipation not just him
a cohort of Filipinos

memorialized citizenship
with a photograph
Dimas-Alang members
who celebrated Philippine
independence unaware
of the consequences of freedom
for them had the widest smiles

in our photograph
we see only Enrique
everyone else cut out
by a daughter who
wanted her daddy
uncomplicated
by history
and other brown
men other faces

she'd have to parse
to extract him from
a community she knew
little of

_____

Language sourced from government documents may be altered to
align with how it's received by impacted populations.

Filipinas in Louisiana

I. NOLA Filipinas
for men born in the Islands
host of second-generation daughters
to imagine settling down with

young American mestizas
resemble Maria Clara
the beauty of Rizal's imagination

but women of Louisiana
barmaids shrimp pickers
maidens of the front porch

raised with jazz and chop suey
big bands and Mardi Gras parades

baked cookies for the St. Joseph's altar
then strolled Canal St. in their Sunday best

drank whiskey at the Manila Bar
and beer in the graveyard

played keno and poker
danced until the band quit

whispered in the ears
of their preening partners
"keep up"
and they would

for they knew more suitors
would disembark
from each ship in port

II. Courtship (Version 1)
"us daughters married
who our fathers selected

men from the old country
Filipino sailors fresh from ships
invited to house parties

all us teenage girls in formal dress
we'd blend like southern society"

III. Courtship (Version 2)
"we'd have parties
dances drink beer

meet up nothing
parents could do

all us teenage
girls ran off

married older
Filipino men

with jobs on ships
we wanted freedom

someone to take
care of us

we were so young
knew no better"

IV. Carnival Queens
big to-do to crown
Miss Philippines
to reign over the
Carnival Ball
sit on the throne
of Mardi Gras

anyone could vote
as many times
as they wanted
for a penny

relatives sent money
orders from around
the country to have
a queen in the family

each week the tally
counted so you knew
how many cents you
needed to move ahead

if not the queen
maid of a Philippine
province
Miss Luzon
Miss Visaya
Miss Mindanao
or the lodge
Miss Dimas-Alang

escorted by
teenaged dukes
grade school pages

each dress decorated
to tell a story
narrated by an emcee
as they waltzed
across the ballroom floor

a prelude for
Mardi Gras day
when thousands
will call and wave
as they parade by

a celebration
to never forget
of being Filipino
and being of
Louisiana

Based on conversations with my grandmother, descriptions in the
diary of Celine Padilla, and interviews with the Burtanog Family
in Hershel A. Franks, Debra M. Stayner, Kenneth R. Jones,
and R. Christopher Goodwin, *Ethnohistory of Filipinos of Southern
Louisiana* (prepared for the US Department of the Interior,
National Park Service, Jean Lafitte National Historical Park,
Louisiana, July 9, 1986), 151–205.

When We Drank at the Filipino Colony Bar (1942-45)

spent the day in town
went to a parade then a dance
had a good time

Hugo's ship came in
we went to the Colony Bar
Nick treated us plenty

went to Charlie's Place
for Filipino music
had a real good time

Toby got a ship out of Mobile
Mr. Johnny and an American
fellow were about to fight

the boys from California left
wasn't any crowd at all
came home early

went to Lafitte cemetery
just like a summer day
drank beer got sunburnt

went to the Colony Bar
had a good time
went to Canal St.

bought my wedding outfit
got home late from the Colony Bar
everybody a good time

Hugo and I went to the show
saw "This Land is Mine"
today Hugo and I got married

everybody a good time
we all went to the Colony
Billy and his boys played

everybody danced
rained almost all day
skipped the Carnival Ball

took a walk to the Colony Bar
wasn't any crowd at all
we left early

Dolores christened her baby today
had a good time at the Colony
Hugo got a job on the Yarmouth

worked all day then to the Colony
had a good time
came home after twelve

Louis treated to the Chop Suey House
I ate fried chicken
Hugo and Angelo shipped out

I slept late
went to the Colony again

Mr. Guillera died today
didn't go to the Colony Bar
it rained all evening

today went to the wake
then to the Colony
it was crowded

had a good time
went to the wake again
walked so much my feet were sore

went to the funeral
really sad
played cards all evening

closed the Colony

supposed to go look for a job but didn't
Polly left for Texas to get a ship
Adong too

went out to the Beach
I won a cat
Hugo a dog

got his vacation money from the base
went by the Golden Eagle
but didn't win

the Colony opened again
had a real good time
today is St. Joseph's Day

didn't go to the altars
played the lottery
didn't hit

today is Easter Sunday went to the Manila Bar
there was a pretty good crowd
had a pretty good time

Eva died today
Hugo and I went to the Colony
then to her wake

Joe Umadhay died today
put him in Eva's place
we all went to the funeral

got a job turning bags
will stick it out a few more days
Hugo and I bought our furniture at Kirschman's

Hugo went to Mobile again
wonder how long he'll be
hope the ship comes here

we went and played keno
none of us hit
ate at Fong's

ironed clothes today
don't believe I can iron tomorrow
because I'm getting tired

today is our anniversary
Hugo isn't here
I didn't go anywhere

went to the Colony Bar
drank so much I passed out
didn't get April-fooled by anyone

had a good time
didn't do any work today
everyone's sad

the invasion in France began
went to the Colony for a while
then crossed the river to visit Mama

played cards all evening
won a few nickels
had a good time

Louis died while across in the Army
couldn't even get a table at the Colony

got a letter from Hugo
he'll be gone a year
went by the Manila Bar

ironed plenty shirts
then walked to the Colony
had plenty of whiskey and beer

a really good time
went to the Three Way
really sleepy when I got home

got a letter from Hugo with some Japanese money
answered it right away
so tired of sewing

I gave a house party
we had a nice crowd

cleaned the house
then took me a nap
Fe Fe set my hair for me

had a good time at the dance
plenty Filipino boys from a ship
really can dance

wish Hugo would hurry and come home
supposed to pick blackberries
but didn't

stayed home and wrote letters
visited Mama
made Italian cakes for Clara

wasn't such a big crowd at the Colony
but we stayed until curfew
Hugo's not home for his birthday

didn't go anywhere
it's awfully
lonesome

slept all evening
went to the Colony Bar
had a good time

Based on entries from the five-year diary (1941–45) of Celine
Padilla, a second-generation Filipino American raised in and
around NOLA who drank at the Filipino Colony Bar operated
by Miguel Guillera (my great-grandfather), who lived above the
bar with his wife, Florence, and for a few years some of their
grandchildren, including my father, his siblings, and the daughter
of Felicia Guillera and Jose Umadhay (my Aunt Caggy).

Barataria Bay

In 1718 this area was not a bay, but rather the Lakes of the Chitimacha, six distinct bodies of water collectively named for the people French colonizers enslaved, killed, and displaced.

Undisclosed Barataria Island

perhaps the first *Filipino colony* established in the United States
was one of many settlements erased from history
in a region where islands succumb
to sea rise and coastal erosion
intriguing coincidence if Manilamen
first settled in the last home of Juan St. Malo's *band of Maroons*
both fleeing injustice from Spanish colonial rule
finding it safer in the *uncivilized* wetlands
where they could fend for themselves
trade with each other
maybe Maroons told Manilamen of the Isle of St. Malo
a paradise of natural resources
Barataria without the smugglers
who navigated pirogues loaded with iron and gin
through narrow bayous to the back door of NOLA
and pirates or if you prefer privateers
who freed sailors from ships
how many Manilamen were stranded at Grand Terre
by Jean Lafitte and his men
perhaps when Augustin Feliciano chose to settle in Barataria Bay circa 1807
it was not to join Lafitte but to be near other Manilamen
perhaps the first Filipino settlement was purposively unnamed
like the place Filipino moss collectors returned to
after their one and only visit to the Grand Isle courthouse (1882)
ended with the matter being resolved over a cold drink at the General Store
a home so indistinct that every story told of it
described numerous inlets and islands
anyone questioned about it revealed little
more than the expectations of their inquisitors
Manilamen employing ambiguity to protect their refuge
from being mapped named and known

Suggested by Augustin Feliciano, the earliest named Filipino to settle in Louisiana—"The Largest Colony of Filipinos in America," *The Filipino*, March 1906.

Encouraged by Charles Silcio, who claimed that "Grand Lake was the original place settled"—*Ethnohistory*, 147.

Endorsed by the experience of a group of Filipino moss collectors—"Curious Judgement," *Times-Picayune*, December 13, 1882.

Raking shrimp on a platform village in Barataria Bay. From Charles Tenney Jackson, *The Fountain of Youth* (New York, Outing Publishing Company, 1914).

When Filipinos Dried Shrimp in Louisiana (1870–1965)

I. Shrimp Drying Platforms
Manila Village Bassa-Bassa
Chung Fat Fifi Island
Camp Dewey Quong Sun
Petit Caillou Clark Cheniere
and more
acres of cypress plank
each built over a low island
each factory and village
each community

starts with fingers strong
and agile enough
to weave seines fine
enough to harvest shrimp

then luggers and labor to stretch nets
down the coast Filipino yes Chinese
Spanish French Italian Croatians
Japanese Mexican African American
Native American Creole
and Cajuns populated
over a hundred platforms
scattered across Barataria Bay

II. Barataria Bay
not a bay but an estuary
framed by abandoned
Mississippi lobes
Lafourche deltas
Des Allemands swamps
to the south Grand Terre
Grand Isle then the Gulf

crustaceans (blue crabs
shrimp) and fish that feed
on them (trout redfish)
abundant alongside
water-loving mammals
(mink otter muskrat)
each seeking optimum
salinity between the Gulf
and fresh to brackish marshes

III. Filipino Villages (1880s–1940s)
Quintin
de la Cruz
built stilted shelters
over oyster beds
called them
Manila Village
more Filipino villages

would follow
Clark Cheniere
more
Cabinash
Clubhouse
Camp Dewey . . .

at the height of the shrimp-
drying industry each sustainable
island etched with stilted shanties
bachelor bunkhouses
dwellings for families

bustling community
in a livable wetland
rain for drinking water
no problem with food

you could fish out
your front door
lots of shrimp
you had deer rabbit
prairie hens greens
grown in raised gardens
rice for a jambalaya

enough to share
sail over for a sinigang
go from one platform
community to another

everything you needed
right there
if not sternwheelers
for regular freight
passage through
interior bayous
to and from NOLA

IV. Seines (1860s–1910s)
in late summer and early fall
when young shrimp outgrow
shallow bayous and inlets
fishermen stretched seines
along the shore waist-deep
(fifteen men to go 200 feet)
shook the lead line
to the sandy bottom
tilted chins above the chop
and eyed the clotted skies

when the circle tightened
redfish and croaker surfaced
flounders slithered underfoot
shrimp gelled into a shimmering mass

the catch secured in the deep pockets
of long-handled dip nets
scooped into straw baskets
topped with Spanish moss
to keep them cool and moist
for the short sail
back to the platforms

V. Profits
each fisherman a share
captain a share
boat a share
seine a share
captain's wife a share
for cooking beans
alternating red and
white

if the captain fair
crews could earn
enough to overwinter
at the edge of the Quarter

VI. Dancing the Shrimp
production began with a boil
baskets of shrimp dipped
into brick-lined vats of brine
then spread across a 100-yard cypress deck
raised so the breeze rustled marsh grass
whistled between boards

in three days of salt air Louisiana sun
105 lbs. of shrimp curled to fifteen

yet not done

attendants raked cured crustaceans
in preparation for the dance
siaui
burlap-covered feet
waltz exoskeletons
each turn
more firm flesh
as shells
dust to bran

no missed steps

guitar or not
they marched
slid tired
jubilant feet
across orange fields

VII. Distribution
in Louisiana a bar snack
like potato chips
good with beer
integrated into gumbos and sautés
or sticky stews of okra
just a few recipes unless
you're Asian enough
to enjoy sea
in almost anything

in chop suey
restaurants
across America
all the dried shrimp
from Barataria Bay

still so much more
to China via NOLA
where Chinese distributors
packed barrels of shrimp
for Hong Kong Shanghai
other East Asian ports

Barataria shrimp in demand
enough shrimp in Asia
and the closer coast of California
not with the concentration
of carotenoids to produce
the tasty orange crescents
caught and dried in Louisiana

VIII. Migrations
Filipinos
from the rest of the US
came South on rumors
of easy pickins

a call repeated in galleys
and markets anywhere
one gathered with
other Filipinos

of kabayans
getting rich
dancing
on shrimp

IX. Clark Cheniere or Clarksville
shell island in Little Lake
a family place with a teacher
midwife number of cypress cottages
general store run by Juan Rojas
the unofficial mayor
one named street
the oak-lined Dewey Ave.
a big hall with poker
played every night
for company matchsticks

and site of another
Filipino platform
the Leon Rojas built
by the son of Juan

sent to NOLA mighty
fine shrimp oysters fish ducks
kept a share for cou'bouillions
jambalaya
vinegared fish eggs
called kinilaw
kept select speckled
trout to salt in barrels
then spread open

on raised racks
until the sun
dried the sea
into them

X. Great Gulf Storm (1893)
swept away season's catch
what will sustain them
as they bury and rebuild

swept away expert dryers
who will measure the sun
and the steps of dancers

swept away fishermen
more will leave
more will come

XI. Shrimp Bill (1906)
who lived meagerly off the marsh
who endured the torrential seasons
who introduced and built the industry

who knows shrimp better
businessmen?
politicians?

who would protect the fisheries
those tramp fishermen from nowhere?

who from the city could benefit?
who from Baton Rouge could cash in?

XII. Trappers
once public marsh
but bought and portioned
by entrepreneurs like Leon Rojas
leased his land to fishermen
who made winters trapping muskrat
spent months in the marsh
some with wife and children
in a rough temporary camp
each morning at the traps
then all day to skin clean and stretch
the smell of drying flesh
enveloped the camp
until Rojas arrived
purchased the pelts
and sold them

XIII. Labor (1911)
America's eyes opened
to child labor the bright freckled
five-year-old who shucks oysters
at Barataria Canning Co.
for fifteen cents a day
any day
he can be convinced

in the trial of J Chung Lee
nine white witnesses told
a story as old as Bayou Defond
shanghaied into labor
secured on a marshy island
no means to escape
forced to fish
to earn their keep

Charlie (Chinese)
spent forty years on platforms
instead of paying him his fair share
immigration called to deport him

XIV. Tropical Storm (1915)
Bassa-Bassa
(low and flat in Chinese)

overwhelmed by waves
before the full fury broke

nothing discerned but small
boats on submerged prairies

those who attempted riverbanks
driven back to wrecked villages

steamer for NOLA
lucky to go aground on a log

distressing cries for help
they could do nothing when waves rose

all still afloat swept into the Gulf

terror-stricken fishermen
women children crowd
into Juan Rojas's store
all tell of terrible loss

crowds along banks
wade with all their
earthly belongings
in shouldered sacks
wait for a way out

XV.
boats not reliant on wind
would tug out four or five
sloop-rigged vessels
some with trailing dinghies
let them all loose
in blue water
to follow gulls
chase shimmering bay-top shadows

XVI. Fisher Brothers
sons of Manila Village
learned the yield of gulf waters
and shrimp drying
from Chinese and Filipinos

took what they could

a lesson learned
by Leon Rojas
whose thick rough
fingers were rarely
compelled to
leave a signature

XVII. No Luck (1916)
Quinton
de la Cruz
lost it all

cards no luck
cockfights less
more debt
how much for the Creole Girl
Viscaya

Good News
how much the general store
all its inventory
the land under Manila Village
docks and all improvements
camps at Cabanish
how much
for this roll
of the dice

XVIII. Jules Fisher (1923)
soon to be senator
Manila Village monarch
new *head of the dried-shrimp industry*
notorious sweatshop owner
friend of the people and Huey Long
whose huge shadow kept labor cheap

good too
Jules gave clothes
food and shelter
to city drunks
bums with nothing
brought them to Manila Village
let them fish it off

XIX. Tourist (1930s)
my grandmother saw
wide empty platforms
couldn't imagine
families lived over the bay
men danced on shrimp

couldn't understand
Manila Village as beacon

too young to value community
too much a part of it to speculate
on who she would be
if her father heard
nothing of a Louisiana
where Filipinos
had their own villages

XX. Trawlers
a whole family'd go about the business of the boat
gas-powered trawlers large enough to roll
through the mountainous waves of the Gulf
family of four could catch as much as a fifteen-man seine crew
wives would do any work their husbands did
and cook and clean and care for the children
who mostly did the sorting separating shrimp
and crabs from a debris of minnows and catfish

XXI. Decline (1930s–40s)
if it wasn't market
disruption (Japan
invades China)
or the threat of storms
it was technology
(powerboats trawls
refrigeration canning
mechanical shrimp shellers)
less labor for more product

in the '40s only seven
platforms remained
all for seasonal work

platform-life moved inland
first women and children

then fishermen seeking better
pay for less strenuous labor

relocated to Lafitte and Harvey
the Latin-side of NOLA
walking distance to the river
French Market
Italian Hall where they'd
dance into the night

XXII. Nostalgia
but all in NOLA pales to golden
dunes dribbling to the Gulf

where we fired wreckage and
danced upon orange crescents

now the smell of dried shrimp
makes us long for a dip in the bay

where we washed the sun-dried
sweat of labor from our faces

and let our young hearts set
on the shores of other islands

National news accounts in 1898–99 conflated St. Malo with
Manila Village, retold the story of one as the other, as if setting —
time and place — doesn't matter.

Newspapers report us through their filters, other us, but we read
them, to fill the gaps in our story we make them our own, minus
the obvious biases, add context, a present perspective, call this
our history.

Aerial view of Manila Village in the 1930s taken by Fonville Winans.
Courtesy of the Winans family.

Manila Village

a substantial capital venture
coinciding with or stimulating
an influx of Filipino migrants
who'd willingly live and labor
above unpredictable seas

a little city
employing up to 700 in the season
ten-square with all the amenities—
housing post office
general store factory
evenings of playing cards

even after Betsy ripped out the platform
still a symbol
after the economic import
of dried shrimp diminished
still an Asian American industry
after fishermen left the water
still the bay Filipinos pioneered
after they raised children for the city
still a beacon still a call to remember

Recipes

Sotanghon

growing up my favorite Filipino dish
"sut-ta-hung" in our NOLA tongue
made with dried shrimp and pork
red gravy and bean threads
English for the Tagalog sotanghon
but we didn't know
not a dish an ingredient
one rarely paired with tomato
sauce the way Granny would
she grew up in the Marigny
where Filipinos held dances at the Italian Hall
baked Italian cookies for the annual St. Joseph's Day feast
perhaps our tomato-based Filipino recipe
originated between porches
between stories of red gravy and pork stew
discussions of all kinds of pasta and noodles
conversations on the proper consistency of sauce
how it should sit on top a bed of spaghetti
would blend with talk about how in the Philippines
noodles were soaked in the sauce
so the flavor was evenly distributed
perhaps these discussions fused into a recipe
brown the cubed pork
add the tomato sauce
season with garlic and pepper
some soy sauce instead of salt
instead of basil add ginger
add those Barataria dried shrimp you snack on
let it simmer
pile the threads into the pot
press them into the liquid
stir until they go limp

serve over rice
a Filipino dish not found in cookbooks
or cooked in the Philippines
or anywhere but Louisiana
where Filipinos dried shrimp
and danced the Italian Hall

Get Your Father from the Bar

he'd spin me on a stool
choose
t-shirted magician
he'd pull a packet
of dried shrimp
from a cap
this
a beef stick from an ear
or this
prop me on the bar
disappear in the smoke of his own stories

he hid in imaginary caves
scenes where palms popped up
climbed coconut trees
all he had to eat and drink
dropped them down
bombs curled to the ground
he grew swift evading a forest
of Japanese soldiers
skilled at dodging enemy attack
he spun
grabbed their attention
swallowed the underbrush
gone

then he'd sing me home
shuffle past raised silent porches
call faces out of windows
tap and slap with sidewalk choristers
knees up he'd say
as I bent up familiar steps
stumbled to the holstered
arms of mother
threw myself around her
before she could draw

Do-bo

adobo which we called "do-bo"
was the other Filipino dish
used to mix up our Sunday routine
of roast pork or beef with mashed potatoes
usually a pork adobo cubed from a pork roast
perhaps a last-minute decision
substitute rice for potatoes
cook the pork into a vinegary stew
sometimes mixed with chicken
but only after chicken was sold without bones
most of the ingredients of a cookbook recipe
meat vinegar soy sauce garlic bay leaf
black peppercorns and sometimes ginger
but our adobo had a little Louisiana kick
a bag of crab boil with coriander and mustard seeds whole
all spice cayenne and dill released into the pot
so the spice berries and seeds cooked into the sauce
you couldn't identify them
until an intense burst of flavor
disrupted the fragile balance of salt and tang
too much for my young palate
not sure who determined adobo
needed Louisiana ingredients
now we use Lola's recipe with the sweet
addition of a spoon or two of cane sugar
to adjust for the creativity of our cooks
and the variety of our vinegars

Become

what we are (work
hard) (adaptable)
negotiates with

what we were
(dropout poor) (under-
employed) (dreams
of [_____])

we value where
we know (city
streets) (southern
suburbs) (barrio)
where we went
(fishing village)

wrap presence
(work) (sleep)
(love) (sorrow)

with our needs
(dress you couldn't afford)
traditions (always open

doors) and comforts
(fresh-baked pandesal)
 we don't forget

we negotiate
what we can be
(labor) (opportunity)
(migrant) (model)
(social construction)

transform (status)
what we came from
(sardines and rice)
(oyster-shelled streets)
(two-stop jeep ride)

anecdotes to shape us
(diligent) (contract
worker) (independent)
position ourselves
(on whose foot)

we (blank stare audience)
(narrative passengers)
can identify (Manilamen)
(American) (Filipino)

(call me [name it])

become what (ancestry)
(heritage) (stereotype)
we were born to be

grasp (culture)
(erasure) (community)
connect when we can
(memory) (history)
(noodle dish we both cook)

become
and become
(secure)
(satisfied)
(unsettled)

Documented

Miguel Guillera (my great-grandfather, second to left) with four other Filipinos on the USS *Kansas*. *Harper's Weekly*, April 10, 1909.

First Filipino Sailors

in the United States Navy
arrived at Hampton Roads in 1909
aboard the USS Kansas
to a welcome unlike any
other immigrants would receive
thousands of spectators
cheering along the shore
President Theodore Roosevelt
hailing his "boys in blue"
amongst them five Filipino
Mess Attendants Third Class
including Miguel Guillera
(second from left
peacoat under an arm)
a year after joining America
on Harper's *Odds and Ends of Interest* page
laid out between the Wright
aeroplane in Paris and a Hawaiian
princess on horseback
highlighting America's ingenuity
and imperial ambitions

I discovered the only photograph we have of my great-grand-
father while reading through articles about the USS *Kansas* to
understand the context of his naval service. Aunt Caggy, who was
five when he died, identified him.

A Filipino American Life in Letters to/from US Institutions

Letters and documents from US government archives — Immigration and Naturalization Services and the military and civil service personnel files of Miguel Guillera — selected, edited, condensed, and (annotated) into a narrative of Miguel Guillera's life in the United States.

Service
(1908)

From: Miguel Guillera
To: US Navy, Naval Station at Cavite, Philippine Islands

I, Miguel Guillera, (a citizen of the Philippines), desiring to enlist in the Navy of the United States (as a Mess Attendant 3c), oblige myself to serve four years from September 10, 1908, and subject myself to the laws, regulations, and disciplines of the Navy.

DESCRIPTIVE LIST.

Age,.....**18**.....years ...**10**.... months; Height,......**5**..... feet......**7**..... inches; Weight,....**124**..lbs.;

Eyes,......**Filipino**......; Hair, ...**Filipino**..........; Complexion,......**Filipino**........

Ambition
(1912)

From: Miguel Guillera, Mess Attendant 2c
To: USS Kansas

1. I respectfully request permission to take the civil service exam for a position as a clerk or day inspector in the custom or Isthmian service (on the Isthmus of Panama facilitating the construction of the Panama Canal).
2. I have been preparing for this examination for the past three years and five months (since my enlistment).
3. My (four year) enlistment will expire September 10, 1912.

From: Miguel Guillera
To: Bureau of Immigration and Naturalization

The Constitution of the US does not give any provision of the entrance of the Filipinos into US citizenship. It's my whole intention to be a US Citizen upon the expiration of my enlistment of four years in the US Navy.

Therefore, I respectfully request further information in regard to this and thanking you in advance.

~~~~

From: Division of Naturalization
To: Miguel Guillera

You are advised that the act of July 25, 1894 provides that any alien who served in the Navy five consecutive years, and has been honorably discharged therefrom, shall be admitted to become a citizen. You will therefore observe that you will not be eligible to file a petition for naturalization, upon the completion of an enlistment of only four years.

The question as to whether a Filipino can be naturalized can be determined only by the court at such time as a position for naturalization is filed and final hearing thereon is had. It may be stated, however, for your information, that a number of courts have held that Filipinos are not eligible for admission to citizenship.

~~~~

From: USS Kentucky
To: Secretary of the Navy

1. It is requested that Miguel Guillera and Manuel Garcia, Mess Attendants, recently honorably discharged from the USS Kansas be transferred to this vessel upon their reenlistment.
2. The men have no assurances that they will remain on board the vessel (or that the vessel will remain stationed in Philadelphia).

(1914)

From: Miguel Guillera, Mess Attendant 1c
To: USS Kentucky

1. It is requested that I be granted permission to take the coming civil service examination for Navy Yard service.
2. My reasons for this request are: I am confident of passing the examination and getting an appointment whereby I shall be able to earn a better living (I have a family to raise and need to earn more money).

~~~~~

From: Chief of Bureau of Navigation

Disapproved, only men serving the last year of their enlistment are permitted to take civil service examinations.

~~~~~

From: Miguel Guillera, Mess Attendant 1c
To: USS Arkansas

I respectfully request that I be permitted to purchase my discharge from the United States Naval Service for the following reasons:

(A) My pay as a Mess Attendant First Class, $27.89 a month, is insufficient to support my family, which includes my wife, child, mother-in-law, and myself

(B) In order to obtain a position in civil life to provide for my wife who has been in poor health and my mother-in-law who is too advanced in age (fifty) to be of financial assistance.

(C) To take the civil service exam (which I am unable to take while enlisted).

~~~~~

From: Bureau of Navigation
To: USS Arkansas

Approved.

To: Bureau of Navigation
From: Recruiting Station

> 1. Guillera called at this office today making the following
>   request: permission to reenlist with a rating of Ward
>   Room Steward.
> 2. He states that the conditions for which he was allowed
>   to purchase his discharge do not exist (he cannot se-
>   cure a better job).

To: Recruiting Station
From: Chief of Bureau of Navigation

If qualified, Guillera may reenlist as Mess Attendant First Class.
The rating of Ward Room Steward is not approved.

Before reenlisting he must sign a statement as follows: "I reenlist
with the understanding that I will not be eligible to purchase my
discharge during the period for which I now enlist."

(1916)

To: US Mint
From: Miguel Guillera

I, Miguel Guillera, do solemnly swear that, to the best of my
knowledge and ability, I will support and defend the Constitu-
tion of the United States against all enemies foreign and domes-
tic; that I will bear true faith and allegiance to the same, and that
I will faithfully and diligently perform the duties of the office of
temporary helper at the United States Mint at Philadelphia. So
help me God.

Opportunity
(1917)
To: Fort Mifflin Naval Ammunition Depot
Subject: (Should we hire Miguel Guillera?)
From: US Mint

My only knowledge of Miguel is through his six months of temporary service, during which period his work was satisfactory.

From: Hospital of the University of Pennsylvania

The inquiry form you sent me concerning Miguel Guillera is almost impossible for me to fill out. The man was an orderly here for some time (sixteen months) and was satisfactory in every respect; doing his work efficiently. The form you sent me calls for much more information than I can possibly and honestly give (I don't know him that well).

From: Hospital of the University of Pennsylvania

He was very willing and ambitious, but he was continually asking for money to be advanced, apparently a poor manager in this respect.

(1918)
To: Fort Mifflin Naval Ammunition Depot
From: Miguel Guillera

I would like to come back to work in the Fort. I left two months ago (for a better opportunity). I was a second-class ordnance man for about eleven months. What I would like to find out is if I can come back as First Class Ordnance. My rating on the Civil Service Eligible List for Sub-inspector of Ordnance is 79% which pays from $4.48 to $5 and up a day.

I would be very glad to come back if you can give me some other kind of position besides second class ordnance man.

Debt
(1921)

To: Miguel Guillera
From: Fort Mifflin Naval Ammunition Depot

This office has been docked $7.45 for overpaying you in 1918.
You were paid for leave at the rate you were getting when paid,
instead of the rate you were getting when on leave. Send the
money with the bearer of this letter.

~~~~

To: Fort Mifflin Naval Ammunition Depot
From: Miguel Guillera

I received your letter informing me of the alleged overpayment. I
don't understand how I could have been overpaid. I always kept
an account of how much I was supposed to get paid. In fact, I was
thinking that I lost a few days vacation. For the fifteen months
that I worked, I was entitled to thirty-six days' vacation with pay
and some sick leave as well.

So, if there was any mistake made, it can't have been on my part.
I would be obliged if you could look this over, as $7.45 is a lot to
a married man with four little children and considering the high
cost of living and the $1,400 a year I make as a government clerk.

~~~~

To: Miguel Guillera
From: Fort Mifflin Naval Ammunition Depot

I will endeavor to make it clear to you just how this overpay-
ment occurred. You were employed at the depot on May 7, 1917.
During the first service year as you know employees are not
allowed to take leave with pay, but leave is earned during this
time which may be taken during the second service year or the
employee may be reimbursed for leave taken without pay during
the first year, later on...

I trust the above explanation will convince you and again request that you send me the amount due ($7.45) immediately.

~~~~

To: Miguel Guillera
From: Fort Mifflin Naval Ammunition Depot

No reply has been received to my letter. An immediate reply is requested, in order that the matter be adjusted as directed by the Auditor of the Navy Department. Check or Money Order should be made payable to the Disbursing Officer, Navy Yard, Philadelphia, Pa., and should be forwarded to Fort Mifflin.

~~~~

To: Philadelphia Post Office
From: Fort Mifflin Naval Ammunition Depot
Subject: Miguel Guillera—postal employee at Central Post Office

1. The subject of the letter was formerly and employee at this Depot.
2. In 1918 he was through error, overpaid the amount of $7.45.
3. A number of communications have been addressed to Guillera, to which no satisfactory reply has been received.
4. It is requested that the Postmaster have this matter brought to the attention of Guillera and that a check or money order for $7.45 be forwarded to this Office.

~~~~

To: Philadelphia Post Office
From: Florence Guillera

I am very sorry my husband was not able to keep his promise by sending the money to Fort Mifflin. I was sick as I am in a delicate state of health (pregnant), so I could not spare the money, but he will certainly send it by the second of next month.

To: Fort Mifflin Naval Ammunition Depot
From: Miguel Guillera

I am sending you the $7.45. I am sorry I could not do it sooner, but my wife was sick and I need the money very badly.

~~~~

To: Miguel Guillera
From: Fort Mifflin Naval Ammunition Depot

Money order for $7.45 in settlement of the amount overpaid to you as wages is hereby acknowledged.

(1925)
To: Postmaster, Philadelphia Post Office
From: Assistant Postmaster, Philadelphia Post Office

Clerk Guillera made application for sick leave with pay on the 23rd instant. This case was investigated and the report of the representative of this office who visited Mr. Guillera's home is as follows: "No one at home; the neighbor across the street advised me that they family was at the seashore."

It is therefore the opinion of this office that Mr. Guillera has attempted to fraudulently secure sick leave with pay, for which reason it is recommended that he show why he should not be removed from the service.

(1926)
To: Philadelphia Post Office
From: Miguel Guillera

Please do not hold my resignation any longer, as I have to get the money or lose everything. My only wish is to pay my debts and shut those people up. They are driving my wife crazy.

To: Miguel Guillera
From: Philadelphia Post Office

Your resignation as a clerk at this office will take effect August 15, 1926. Kindly call upon the cashier in order to fill out the necessary form to withdraw the money paid into your retirement.

To: Philadelphia Post Office
From: Miguel Guillera

Since I left the post office, it has been a real hardship for my wife and children, as I have not had a decent job. What I know from the post office is of no use outside, so please take me back. I promise to do my best and remain with you. My financial obligations are attended to, and I will no longer contract debts more than I will earn.

To: Philadelphia Post Office
From: Florence Guillera

Pardon me for writing this letter, but I would very much like to know if my husband, Miguel Guillera, has any chance to be reinstated. He has a family of six children. Since he has not worked since he left you, it is getting very hard to get along now. I really do not know what to do as things have gotten to such a crisis now. Please let me know as soon as possible what you can do.

To: Florence Guillera
From: Postmaster, Philadelphia Post Office

I regret to state that the record of Miguel Guillera at this office was unsatisfactory. Therefore there is no chance for his reinstatement.

Miguel left the service under a cloud, owing many merchants and firms for merchandise purchased, and claimed he was resigning to collect his pension in order to pay his numerous debts. We tried to persuade him not to resign and to take other means to settle his debts.

~~~

To: Postmaster, Philadelphia Post Office
From: Superindendent of Mails

After careful consideration of this employee's previous record, this office would interpose no objection to his reinstatement with a favorable recommendation.

~~~

To: Philadelphia Post Office
From: Miguel Guillera

I am sending you receipts and statements from the people who had claims on me. I hope you will consider my reinstatement soon, as my children are on the way to starvation. My rent is two weeks overdue, no coal in the home, and I can't find any kind of work. My children have no shoes to go to school.

(1927)
From: Postmaster, Philadelphia Post Office
To: US Post Office

In view of the efficient service performed by Miguel, it is recommended that his reinstatement as senior substitute clerk be authorized.

To: Philadelphia Post Office
From: Miguel Guillera

I am compelled to decline the position of substitute clerk, foot of roll, as I am positive of the unfairness of the appointment. I believe I deserve an appointment one grade below where I was at the time my resignation was tendered. My long service in the US Navy and civil service does not justify starting at the bottom again.

~~~

To: Miguel Guillera
From: Postmaster, Philadelphia Post Office

I note your statement that you feel this reinstatement is unjust on account of your veteran status. We have many substitutes, about 50% of them ex-service men. Clerks who have resigned for personal reasons have had their opportunity and left the service. If all the reinstatements went to the top of the list, substitutes would never be appointed. They are just as much entitled to consideration and anxious to be appointed as you.

Migration
(1927)

To: Miguel Guillera
From: Postmaster, Philadelphia Post Office

You can be reinstated in New Orleans. Therefore, you should make your application direct to the postmaster at that office.

~~~~

To: US Navy
From: Miguel Guillera

Please kindly give me a copy of my discharge papers. I mislaid my original and need it very badly to get reinstated to the postal service in New Orleans.

(1930)

To: Prohibition Bureau
From: Miguel Guillera

I served as an undercover prohibition agent attached to the Tenth Prohibition District in New Orleans from Sept. 1927 to 1928. During this time, my record will show that I had very close to 1,000 cases from the following cities: New Orleans, Mobile, Pensacola, Baton Rouge, and Bogalusa.

I am a married man with five young children, a hard-working wife, and about nineteen years of government experience. Having been employed by the following departments: six years in the US Navy as a mess attendant and steward, two years in the Navy Yard as an ordnance inspector, two years with the US Shipping Board as a timekeeper, six years with the Post Office as a clerk, one year with the US Mint as a roller of gold and silver, and one year as a prohibition agent. I am now employed by US Steel as a chief steward on one of their ships (out of Mobile). I would be very much obliged if you would consider my reinstatement; It will bring me closer to my family. I am away from them now and most all the time.

To: Philadelphia Post Office
From: Miguel Guillera

I have been in New Orleans over three years and have not found a regular position. So, I have decided for the sake of my wife and the children to try to get back to government service where I have served faithfully for nineteen years. If given the chance, I will remain in service and faithfully serve the government.

Citizenship
(1940)

PHILIPINO COLONY BAR
~~GROCERY~~ AND REFRESHMENT CO.
NEW ORLEANS, LOUISIANA
1107 St. Anthony St.

To: US Navy
From: Miguel Guillera, Proprietor, Filipino Colony Bar, New Orleans
Subject: (Am I a US citizen?)

I enlisted in the US Navy in 1908 when the first lot of Filipinos were taken into the service. I served on the USS Kansas for the whole four years of my enlistment, was honorably discharged Sept. 10, 1912.

On Oct. 29, 1912, I reenlisted for four years. I was stationed on the USS Kentucky in Philadelphia until I was sent to Mexico on the USS Sacramento for occupation (of Vera Cruz) and we stayed there about six months, and I was transferred to the USS Arkansas. Then we sailed for Brooklyn Navy Yard. Then about Oct. 1914, I purchased the balance of my enlistment because my family was growing large. I was given Hon. Dis. again.

Just before, I was first Hon. Disc. on the USS Kansas, I had applied for my US Citizenship, but I never got my papers somehow, and of course I am in doubt of my citizenship. I am asking you, Sir, if I can get my papers through the Navy.

I was brought here by the US Navy, came of age in the US, neither my father nor I have sworn allegiance to Spain (or any other country). I haven't returned to the Islands since I left in 1908, nor have I traveled outside of the US (but with the Navy). I have served the US civil government for thirteen years by way of US civil service examinations and appointments, besides the six years of Naval Service.

I have always believed and considered myself a US citizen.

To: Miguel Guillera
From: Chief of Bureau of Navigation

Our records contain no information regarding your citizenship papers. It will be necessary for you to communicate with the Bureau of Immigration and Naturalization, Department of Justice.

~~~~

To: Bureau of Immigration and Naturalization
From: Miguel Guillera, Proprietor, Filipino Colony Bar, New Orleans

> Please kindly give me some information in regardst to my status, as I have always believed myself to be a US citizen for the following reasons:
>
> When the US Naval Fleet went to Manila in Sept. 1908 about 1,500 or more English educated young Filipinos were wanted by her for Mess Attendant work. I was one of those Filipinos.
>
> I have served the US government both Naval and Civil for eighteen years.
>
> I moved to New Orleans in 1927 and was appointed to the Prohibition Bureau in New Orleans as an undercover prohibition agent. I got into trouble after a year. One of the biggest bootleggers in New Orleans framed me up for a supposed accepted bribe. I was given a year and day for this, and sent to Atlanta, Ga. (federal penitentiary), and was pardoned by President Coolidge. All of my government records are very good and clean except this last one.

Your advice will be greatly appreciated, as I am anxious to do what is right and obtain my citizenship papers. I have a big family and my children are grown up and of voting age.

To: Miguel Guillera
From: Special Assistant to the Attorney General

It is noted you are Filipino, and that you have served with the US
Navy for a number of years. You are informed that persons of the
Filipino race are ineligible for citizenship, except for the classes
set forth on the attached form. Unless you have been naturalized
under this provision of law, you apparently are not a citizen of the
United States.

Brown

Miguel left the Philippines at eighteen
joined the US Navy for a better life
became "American" spoke English well
married an English woman
who called him Michael
had citizen children
quoted from the Constitution
worked for the US government for eighteen years
taught Spanish on the side
worked hard yet willing to call in sick
to take his family to the beach
swore allegiance to the United States
registered for the draft twice
paid his debts went to church
expressed his ambition to climb the economic ladder
became a *star undercover agent* in the Prohibition Bureau
spent several months in a federal penitentiary
a strike against his model immigrant narrative
for accepting a $20 bribe
but pardoned by President Calvin Coolidge
opened a bar
organized in the community
what more could a Filipino do
to become an American citizen

NOTHING

US imperial policies included Filipino land and labor
not citizenship
the US provided Filipinos with passports to designate
them Americans in the eyes of other nations not in the US
where Filipinos were nationals
swore permanent allegiance to a country that didn't want them
President William McKinley publicly stated
I didn't want the Philippines then implemented a policy

of *benevolent assimilation* to *educate . . . and uplift*
and civilize and Christianize Filipinos
Miguel understood the mission
learned English
enlisted in the US Navy
served the United States
surely evidence he was or could be assimilated
but assimilation a bar first-generation Asians aren't meant to clear
Miguel's attempts to petition for citizenship challenged by policies
that intentionally limit processes
that reverberated with nativist calls of *no Filipinos allowed*
another year of service required
a little more proof
another document
amplified by gatekeepers who wouldn't equally
attend to *persons of the Filipino race*
nothing Miguel

ALONE

could have done to successfully navigate the bureaucracy
to become a US citizen
he needed advocates
unbiased processes
the political will of a unified people
something witnessed in the community's efforts
to fight the Merchant Marine Act of 1936
which questioned the loyalty of Filipinos residing in the US
questioned whether they would be a threat to national defense
made clear to Filipinos that their status
both *nationals* and *aliens*
left them vulnerable to punitive policies
made it clear no matter their allegiances
Filipino Americans were not American enough for some Americans
Filipino served as a racial marker to question
loyalty and fitness for inclusion
little brown brother

as colonial subject
labor migrant
not American
I'd like to think Miguel had enough of the illusion
that when he registered his grandson
my father Ronald Gonzales BROWN
instead of WHITE
he did so to end the charade
record it right
stop pretending you can change your race
let the boy know he should be proud
of his Filipino heritage
America will see what it wants to see
he could be American and be brown
like his ancestors
like him before he
thought he could be white

About the Author

Randy Gonzales is a poet, writer, and community historian invested in telling the story of Filipino Louisiana. Born and raised in New Orleans with little knowledge of his Filipino roots, he has worked to reclaim and share the culture and history of Filipino Louisiana. Randy is an associate professor of English at the University of Louisiana at Lafayette, where he holds the Dr. James Wilson/BORSF Eminent Scholar Endowed Professorship in Southern Studies. He holds a PhD in English with an emphasis in poetry from the Center of Writers at the University of Southern Mississippi. As an officer with the Philippine Louisiana Historical Society, Randy wrote the text for the historical marker to commemorate the Filipino settlement at St. Malo. He has been interviewed extensively and given numerous local, regional, and national talks on Filipino Louisiana. You can find out more about Filipino Louisiana at www.filipinola.com and more about Randy at www.randygonzales.com.